For my children and yours,
may you find your wings and have the courage to fly.

My husband,
for your eternal faith, thank you.

My mother Jane,
I aspire to one day become the eternal optimist you were…. We miss you!

Butterfly Rhythm
© 2008 – Leticia Colon de Mejias
Printed in United States of America (USA)
Published by Great Books 4 Kids
(http://www.greatbooks4kids.org)

Butter, the caterpillar, was crawling around.
She was feeding off anything low to the ground.

Not too selective,
You can't blame her though.
She could not see much.
She was down too low.

Butter ate and climbed up a tree.
She climbed and she climbed, and now she could see.

The leaves were much greener.
She ate them up fast,
Munching on knowledge and growing at last.

Butter was confused.
Not quite sure who she was,
She decided to rest.
She was cocooned by love.

Not knowing the outcome,
Not running the show,
When butter woke up,
She'd know where to go.

Butter opened her eyes and set herself free. "This cocoon is too small. I need to be me!"

Butter paused a moment, and opened her wings.
Now Butterfly flies and Butterfly sings.

Butterfly grown
Butterfly free
Butterfly Beautiful
Butterfly is me!

Butterfly Rhythm
Butterfly free
Butterfly flies
But she does not flee

Butterfly Happy
Butterfly Live
Butterfly has so much to Give!

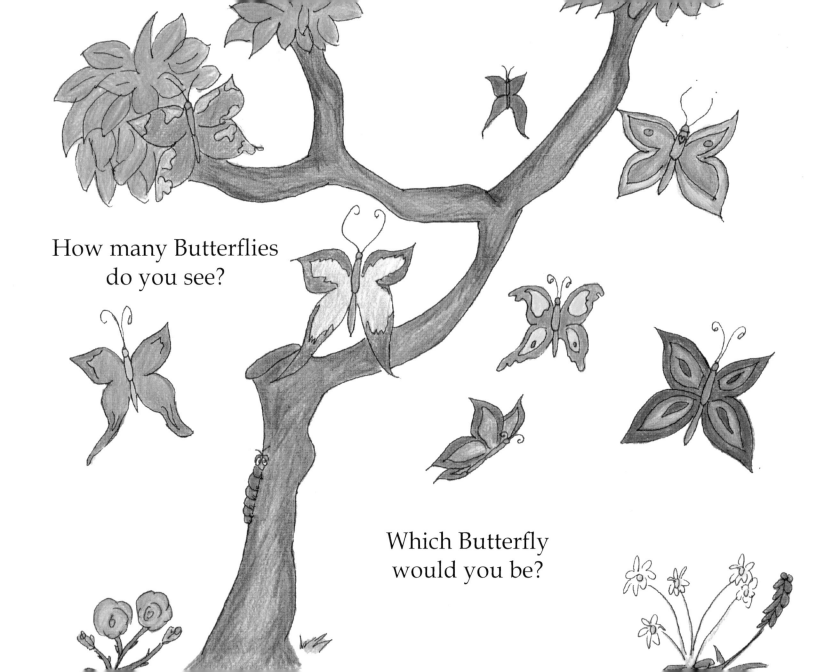

How many Butterflies
do you see?

Which Butterfly
would you be?

Metamorphosis

LIFE STAGES

Butterflies go through four different life stages.
These changes are called metamorphosis.

Egg Stage - A butterfly starts its life as an egg.

Butterfly eggs come in many shapes and colors.

The egg shapes are normally circular ◯,

oval ◯, or pod-shaped ◯.

The egg colors are normally white, green, or yellow.

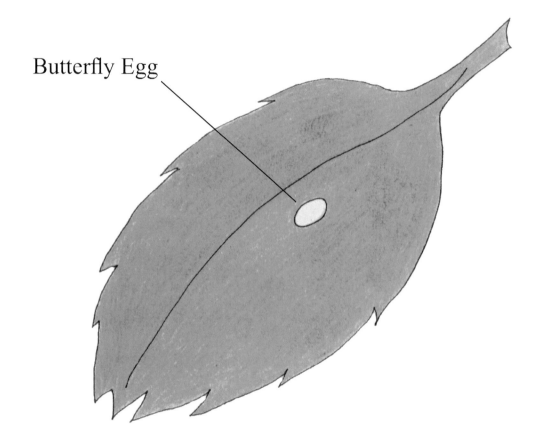

Butterfly Egg

What color and shape is this Butterfly egg?

Larva Stage - larva is sometimes called a caterpillar.

Larva hatch from an egg and eat leaves. The larva stage lasts from two weeks to about a month.

As the larva grows, it sheds its old skin and grows new skin. This is called molting.

Parts of a Caterpillar

Head - The head is the part of the butterfly that holds the brain, eyes, mouth and two antennae.

Eyes - The caterpillar has simple eyes. These eyes are called Ocelli and look like small spots.

Jaws - Caterpillar mouths are called (mandibles). They have very sharp cutting surfaces that easily chop leaves. Underneath the mandible are the two maxillae, small mouth parts that guide the food into the mouth.

Thorax - The thoracic legs are attached to the thorax.

Spiracles - The caterpillar breathes through holes in its side called spiracles.

Abdomen - The prolegs are attached to the abdomen.

Larva

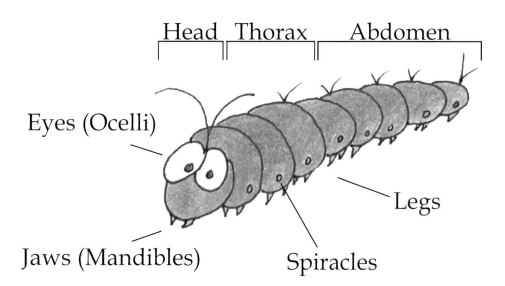

Head   Thorax   Abdomen

Eyes (Ocelli)

Jaws (Mandibles)

Spiracles

Legs

What is another name for Larva?

Pupa Stage - The larva forms a protective shield called a pupa.

The pupa is sometimes called the **chrysalis** or **cocoon**.

In the pupa, the larva is changing into an butterfly.

During the pupa stage, the butterfly is growing its wings.

About a day before the butterfly comes out, the pupa becomes clear and you can see the butterfly inside.

Pupa

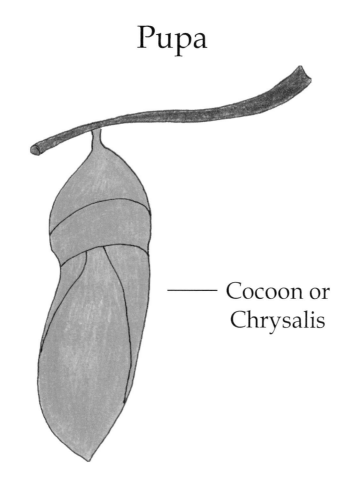

—— Cocoon or Chrysalis

What is another name for Pupa?

Butterfly - Butterfies will continue the life cycle by laying eggs.

Parts of a Butterfly

Head - The head is the part of the butterfly that holds the brain, eyes, mouth and two antennae.

Antennae - Butterflies have two antennae. Antennae are used for smell and balance.

Eyes - Butterflies have two eyes that are made up of many lenses.

Proboscis - Butterflies sip nectar using a spiral, straw-like tongue located on their head.

Thorax - The thorax is the body section between the head and the abdomen. The legs and wings attach to the thorax.

Fore wings - The fore wings are the two upper wings.

Hind wing - The hind wings are the two lower wings.

Legs - All butterflies have six legs.

Abdomen - The abdomen is the segmented tail area of an insect .

Butterfly

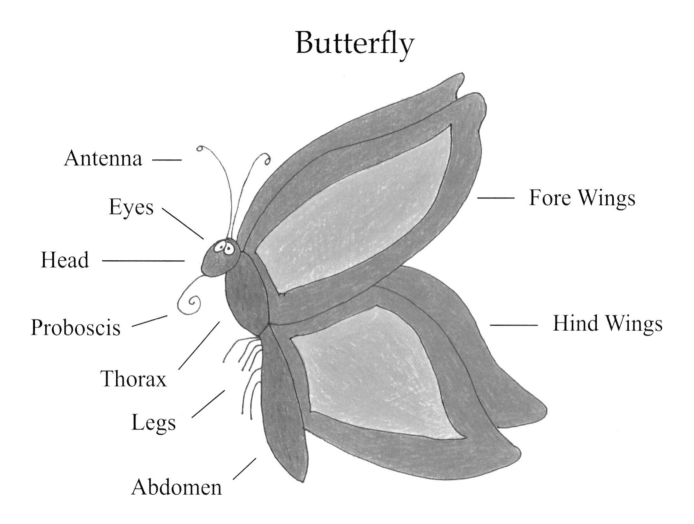

Antenna —

Eyes

Head —

Proboscis —

Thorax

Legs

Abdomen

Fore Wings

Hind Wings

What do butterflies lay?

About the Author

Leticia Colon de Mejias lives in Windsor, Connecticut, with her husband, five children, father, and their dog, Bio-diesel. She writes her books for all children, ranging from newborns to adults. Her stories hold messages we are familiar with and desire to keep close to our hearts. These beautifully illustrated children's stories help us pass our life lessons happily from one generation to the next.

With no hidden agendas, Leticia shares inspirational tales that project ideas of seeking truth, trying your best, helping others, putting your best foot forward, and following your heart. You will be proud to give these books as gifts to your friends and family to encourage them to follow their hearts and dreams.

Other books written by this Author

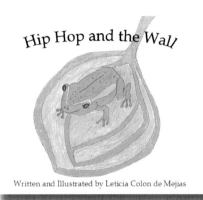

Hip Hop and the Wall

Written and Illustrated by Leticia Colon de Mejias

Hip Hop the Frog journeys to the world beyond his small pond. Along the way he meets new friends. He over comes barriers and learns that he has a secret talent. Hip Hop's travels reveal important lessons about overcoming obstacles blocking his path. Hip Hop demonstrates, "When the going get's tough, the tough get going." This story teaches children to believe in themselves and keep moving forward. You can proudly give this book as a gift to a loved one to encourage her to follow her dreams.

Mrs. Busy Bee

Written and Illustrated by Leticia Colon de Mejias

Mrs. Busy Bee is always BUZZ BUZZ BUZZING about. With the help of a friendly Butterfly, She and her children learn the meaning of "stopping to smell the flowers", and "taking the time to appreciate the little things in life." This story holds lessons about life, love, family, and listening to the quiet voice within us. It reminds us to take the time to care for ourselves and our dreams. This heart warming story is a classic for today's children and adults living a hurried world.